My Mother
Always Used
to Say
That Too...

You can never give a
child too much love or
too many kisses.

A.T.

My Mother Always Used to Say That Too...

Anna Tochter

Angus&Robertson
An imprint of HarperCollins*Publishers*

Angus&Robertson
An imprint of HarperCollins*Publishers*, Australia

First published in Australia in 1999
Reprinted in 1999
by HarperCollins*Publishers* Pty Limited
ACN 009 913 517
A member of the HarperCollins*Publishers* (Australia) Pty Limited Group
http://www.harpercollins.com.au

HarperCollins*Publishers*
25 Ryde Road, Pymble, Sydney NSW 2073, Australia
31 View Road, Glenfield, Auckland 10, New Zealand
77–85 Fulham Palace Road, London W6 8JB, United Kingdom
Hazelton Lanes, 55 Avenue Road, Suite 2900, Toronto, Ontario M5R 3L2
and 1995 Markham Road, Scarborough, Ontario M1B 5M8, Canada
10 East 53rd Street, New York NY 10022, USA

National Library Cataloguing-in-Publication data:

Tochter, Anna.
   My mother always used to say that too – .
   ISBN 0207 19912 4.
   1. Mothers – Quotations. I. Title.
082.0852

Cover photography by Robert Reichenfeld
Teacup on cover courtesy Karen Cooper

Typeset in Cochin 12/15
Printed in Australia by Australian Print Group on 135gsm Glopaque

8 7 6 5 4 3 2
03 02 01 00 99

Dedication

To my grandmother and my mother,
but especially to my children,
Elizabeth and Henry, for
giving me so many opportunities

Contents

❧ Introduction ❧ Please and Thank You ❧

❧ Silence is Golden ❧ Confession is Good for the Soul… ❧

❧ Home is Where the Heart is ❧ Nice Girls Don't… ❧

❧ Mysterious Wisdom ❧ Cleanliness is Next to Godliness ❧

❧ The Price of Motherhood is Eternal Vigilance ❧

❧ The Written Word ❧ Suitors ❧

❧ *Extremely* Unsuitable Suitors ❧ Heartbreak ❧

❧ Maternal Gems ❧ Family Planning ❧

❧ Maternal Martyrdom ❧ Sanctuary ❧ Memories ❧

❧ Household Fairies ❧ The Lovely April in her Prime… ❧

❧ Maternal Flagellation ❧ The Mysteries of Life ❧

❧ Maternal Independence ❧ Maternal Economics I ❧

❈ Maternal Economics II ❈ Maternal Economics III ❈

❈ Don't Say… ❈ A Sense of Humour ❈ I'm Bored… ❈

❈ Maternal Support ❈ Emergency Measures ❈

❈ A Wise Precaution ❈ Warm Words ❈ Any Requests? ❈

❈ Any Requests in Other People's Houses ❈ Family Codes ❈

❈ Comfort in Gossip ❈ The Art of Delegation ❈

❈ The Demon Drink ❈ Maternal Tales ❈ No You Can't… ❈

❈ If a Job's Worth Doing… ❈ Deaf Wish ❈

❈ In My Day… ❈ The Modern Education System ❈

❈ Homework ❈ Yes, My Darling Son ❈

❈ Night-time ❈ Always Look on the Bright Side ❈

❈ Naughty Little Girl to Disobey ❈

❈ Yes, My Darling Daughter ❈ The Good Mother ❈

❈ Mother's Day ❈ The Last Word ❈

Introduction

Six years have passed since I wrote my first book of motherly sayings. In that time, I have been amazed by just how universal these words of maternal practice seem to be. The book has sold in many different countries — all over the world, mothers are chanting some variant of 'least said soonest mended', 'no one's good enough for my daughter', 'where did you leave it?' and so on.

My children are six years older now, allowing me a greater, and seemingly inexhaustible, range of generational wisdom. This new collection of classic (and often contradictory) sayings is another reminder that so much of mothering is like walking upstairs and downstairs at the same time.

My daughter is now in training to be a teenager.
I wonder when the switch came from being sent
to her room as a punishment to never coming out of
it at all. My son promises he will never marry,
which is fine by me, as clearly no one will be good
enough for him either.

The final comforting, yet daunting, development is
that I have moved from borrowing and customising
my mother's sayings, to having those of my own
(at least according to my children).
The metamorphosis is complete – I have *become*
my mother. And I am well satisfied.

Anna Tochter

What do girls do who haven't any mothers
to help them through their troubles?

LOUISA MAY ALCOTT
LITTLE WOMEN

11

Please and Thank You

I didn't hear the magic word...

Silence is Golden

Better to keep your mouth shut and have
everyone think you a fool, rather than open
your mouth and confirm it

›‹•›‹·०·›‹•›‹

Speak up, don't mumble!

›‹•›‹·०·›‹•›‹

Shush, do you want everyone to hear?

›‹•›‹·०·›‹•›‹

There's no need to shout, I'm not deaf!

Confession is Good for the Soul...

Mothers — they get you coming, they get you going. Why do they always have to know everything?

A penny for your thoughts

⊱⊱⊷⊙⊶⊰⊰

If you can't tell *me*, who can you tell?

⊱⊱⊷⊙⊶⊰⊰

Spit it out!

⊱⊱⊷⊙⊶⊰⊰

Keep your thoughts to yourself

⊱⊱⊷⊙⊶⊰⊰

Some things are better left unsaid

Home is Where the Heart is

A child enters your home and makes so much noise
for 20 years that you can hardly stand it: then departs,
leaving the house so silent that you think you will go mad.

JOHN ANDREW HOLMES

I'm changing the locks when you're eighteen

Hello stranger

So, couldn't you have telephoned?

Nice Girls Don't…

get in the front of taxis

▸◂▸─◌─◂▸◂

check out the labels on presents

▸◂▸─◌─◂▸◂

make the first move

17

Mysterious Wisdom

Many a mickle makes a muckle

Cleanliness is Next to Godliness

Brush your teeth and your tongue
three times a day

❧

There's no substitute for clean fingernails

❧

Is that a real wash, or just a
lick and a promise?

19

The Price of Motherhood is Eternal Vigilance

Where have you been till this time of night?

⊱•✦•⊰

I know what you've been doing

⊱•✦•⊰

Have you been with a boy?

What's that on your neck?

⊢·⊹·०·⊹·⊣

I can't sleep till I know you're home

⊢·⊹·०·⊹·⊣

I heard you come in at 2am

⊢·⊹·०·⊹·⊣

You can't lie to me, I'm your mother

The Written Word

Never write down in private what you're not
prepared to have read out in public

Diary keeping – don't

Love letters – make sure you
get them back

Suitors

Do I know him?

>-+-•-0-•-+-<

Do I know his parents?

>-+-•-0-•-+-<

Why can't you bring him home – are you ashamed of us?

>-+-•-0-•-+-<

What does he do for a living?

>-+-•-0-•-+-<

Is that a real job?

Extremely Unsuitable Suitors

He's not good enough for you

▸┼◆─0─◆┼◂

You're throwing yourself away

▸┼◆─0─◆┼◂

He'll never amount to anything

▸┼◆─0─◆┼◂

If brains were dynamite
he couldn't blow his hat off

He couldn't lie straight in bed

Bad blood will out, you mark my words

Don't say I didn't warn you

Well, don't come crying to me

*H*eartbreak

He's not the only pebble on the beach

▸┼◂▸┼◂

You're better off without him

Maternal Gems

Pearls are unlucky

⊱━•◦•━⊰

Rubies are common

⊱━•◦•━⊰

Diamonds should be washed in gin

Family Planning

Never fill up a house with boys trying
for a girl, or vice versa

Maternal Martyrdom
(sometimes known as the Burnt Chop Syndrome)

No, it's fine, I've eaten

‣⊷⊶○⊷⊶◃

You have the last piece

‣⊷⊶○⊷⊶◃

Of course I don't mind

*S*anctuary

No, I haven't been in your room

I just went in to clean it

I haven't been through your personal things

No, I would never read your diary, darling,
I didn't even know you kept one

The wardrobe is for clothes not the floor

How can you live like this?

At *least* make your bed

You'd forget your head if it wasn't screwed on

Memories

You were such a beautiful baby,
I don't know what happened

Household Fairies

Have you tried looking in the wardrobe?
The laundry fairy may have ironed it and hung it up

⊷•⊶

No, I don't know what's for dinner.
The cooking fairy has been at work all day

33

The Lovely April
of Her Prime…

Thou art thy mother's glass, and she in thee
Calls back the lovely April of her prime

WILLIAM SHAKESPEARE
SONNETS 3

I know you find it hard to imagine,
but I was once considered good-looking

⊢⊶⊙⊷⊣

Childbirth ruined my figure

Maternal Flagellation

Where did I go wrong?

Ⓗ

I've been too soft with you, that's been the problem

Ⓗ

I'm just a fool to myself

The Mysteries of Life

Where did you last see it?

Can't you think of anyone but yourself?

Maternal Independence

I'm tired of being taken for granted

┣━◆━०━◆━┫

I won't always be here to do this for you, you know

┣━◆━०━◆━┫

It's time you stood on your own two feet

┣━◆━०━◆━┫

You'll be the death of me

Maternal Economics I

Save the wrapping paper

Maternal Economics II

Keep the string

Maternal Economics III

Penny wise, pound foolish

⊢⊶⊙⊷⊣

Champagne taste and beer income

⊢⊶⊙⊷⊣

Money comes to money

Don't Say...

couch

▸◦◦◦◦◃

ta

▸◦◦◦◦◃

toilet

▸◦◦◦◦◃

beg yours

▸◦◦◦◦◃

pardon

A Sense of Humour

Once is funny, twice is not,
three times deserves a slap

————

You'll be laughing on the other side of your face
when I've finished with you

I'm Bored...

If you're bored, you're boring

Maternal Support

It's just puppy fat

⊢⊶⊙⊶⊣

You'll grow out of it

⊢⊶⊙⊶⊣

No boy wants to date a broom handle

⊢⊶⊙⊶⊣

Nobody will love you like your mother

Emergency Measures

Turn it inside out

Don't take the jacket off

A Wise Precaution

Take a cardigan

Warm Words

Children don't feel the cold

If you're cold, put a jumper on

You'll catch your death of cold
going out dressed like that

Are you sure you'll be warm enough?

Any Requests?

Any more for any more?

▸┼◉┄◉┄◉┼◂

Those that ask don't get; and those
that don't ask, don't want

▸┼◉┄◉┄◉┼◂

'I want' never gets

The discontented child cries for toasted snow

ARAB PROVERB

47

Any Requests in Other People's Houses

Don't ask for seconds

Family Codes

FHB – Family Hold Back (when there
isn't enough to go around)

⊳⊶⊶⊶⊲

HKLP – Holds Knife Like Pen

⊳⊶⊶⊶⊲

HFLC – Holds Fork Like Cello

⊳⊶⊶⊶⊲

PDLE – *pas devant les enfants* (not in front of the children)

Comfort in Gossip

While they're talking about you, they're leaving
some other poor fool alone

⊱─❖─◦─❖─⊰

At least they're talking about you

⊱─❖─◦─❖─⊰

A lady only appears in the newspaper three times
—birth, marriage and death. Anything else is vulgar

The Art of Delegation

It's no good keeping a dog
and barking yourself

The Demon Drink

Never drink on an empty head

⊱┄◦┄⊰

That's not a lady's drink

⊱┄◦┄⊰

Gin makes you depressed, whisky makes you drunk
and vodka makes you anybody's

⊱┄◦┄⊰

Never leave your drink unattended — a man can slip
something into it and take advantage of you

Maternal Tales

Who started this?

――◆―○―◆――

I want the truth, now…

――◆―○―◆――

Don't tell tales

――◆―○―◆――

A slap for the tale and a slap for the teller

Oh what a power is motherhood

EURIPIDES

No You Can't…

More examples of up the down staircase

You're too young

▸┅◈┅◈┅◂

When you're older

▸┅◈┅◈┅◂

Not at your age

▸┅◈┅◈┅◂

You'll be grown up soon enough

Stay a child as long as you can

Don't wish your life away

You're not a baby any more, you know

Grow up – you're not a child

If a Job's Worth Doing…

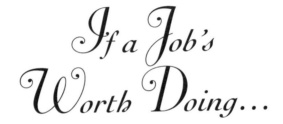

Do it right the *first* time

Deaf Wish

Are you listening to me?

>-+-●-0-●-+-<

Honestly, it all goes in one ear and out the other

>-+-●-0-●-+-<

It's like talking to a brick wall

In My Day…

*Your mother's always wrong; that's why they
made her your mother*

BRUCE JAY FRIEDMAN

I was young myself once you know,
when dinosaurs roamed the earth

＞━◆━◇━◆━＜

Don't take that tone of voice with *me*, young lady

＞━◆━◇━◆━＜

I wouldn't have dared to speak
to *my* mother like that

There's no need to swear

Sarcasm is the lowest form of wit

When I want your opinion, I'll ask for it

In *my* day we didn't answer back

Well, if you're going to take that attitude,
there's no point in discussing it

59

The Modern Education System

Don't they teach you *anything*
at school nowadays?

Two and two makes four — at least it did
when I went to school

Homework

Have you done your homework?

>-I-<I>-O-<O>-I-<

Are you sure? Fine, then you can play

>-I-<I>-O-<O>-I-<

Darling, why did you wait till this morning
to tell me the project on the great artists
of the Renaissance was due today?

Yes, My Darling Son

Begin, baby boy, to recognise
your mother with a smile

VIRGIL
ECLOGUES

No one will ever be good enough for you

Leave it alone, it's not a toy

You're just like your father

You don't get that from *my* side of the family

Night-time

Why aren't you in bed?

╺┉━◆━◇━┉╸

Eating late at night will give you nightmares

╺┉━◆━◇━┉╸

Only children with a bad conscience can't sleep

╺┉━◆━◇━┉╸

If I have to come upstairs once more,
there will be serious trouble

Always Look on the Bright Side

Misery loves company

›─┼─‹◊›─◊─‹◊─┼─‹

It'll seem better in the morning

›─┼─‹◊›─◊─‹◊─┼─‹

It's always darkest before the dawn

›─┼─‹◊›─◊─‹◊─┼─‹

Try and find some good in all this

Δ·I·Φ·O·Φ·I·Δ

This will make you a better person

Δ·I·Φ·O·Φ·I·Δ

I won't say I told you so

Δ·I·Φ·O·Φ·I·Δ

Never mind, have a good cry

Naughty Little Girl to Disobey

My mother said, I never should
Play with the gypsies in the wood
If I did, she would say
'Naughty little girl to disobey'

What did I tell you?

⊢•←○•←○•←•⊣

I said it would end in tears

⊢•←○•←○•←•⊣

I don't find any satisfaction in being right
all the time, you know

66

Yes, My Darling Daughter

Mother may I go and bathe?
Yes, my darling daughter
Hang your clothes on yonder tree,
but don't go near the water

You can go to the party
but I want you home by ten

The Good Mother

*Everybody knows that a good mother gives her children
a feeling of trust and stability. She is their earth. She is
the one they can count on for the things that matter
most of all. She is their food and their bed and their
extra blanket when it grows cold in the night; she is
their warmth and their health and their shelter; she is
the one they want to be near when they cry.*

My Mother Always Used to Say That Too...

She is the only person in the whole world or in a whole lifetime who can be these things to her children. There is no substitute for her. Somehow even her clothes feel different to her children's hands from anybody else's clothes. Only to touch her skirt or her sleeve makes a troubled child feel better.

KATHARINE BUTLER HATHAWAY
THE JOURNALS AND LETTERS OF THE LITTLE LOCKSMITH

Mother's Day

It's children's day every day, today's *my* day

It's lovely darling. What *is it* exactly?

I'll use it every day

Is a simple cup of tea in bed
too much to ask?

The Last Word

When *you're* the Mummy you can
have children of your own to be horrible to,
but for the moment, it's my turn